Affiliate Marketing Mastery

How to Create a Profitable Online Business

Table of Contents

Chapter 1. Introduction

Discover the secrets of successful online entrepreneurship with our special report: "Affiliate Marketing Mastery: How to Create a Profitable Online Business". Unlock the potential to generate an impressive income stream, regardless of your previous experience or knowledge. This comprehensive guide brims with cheerful step-by-step instructions, insider tips, and proven strategies to ensure your success. It offers a persuasion powerful enough to transform any novice into a profitable affiliate marketer. Are you ready to take the first step towards financial freedom and independence? Grab this golden opportunity to embolden your future with affiliate marketing mastery. This report is your ticket to an exciting journey through the dynamic world of online entrepreneurship. Let's make your business dreams a reality!

Chapter 2. Unlocking the Mystery of Affiliate Marketing

Affiliate marketing is a powerful vehicle that many individuals and businesses use to expand their online income capabilities. With its roots in traditional referral marketing, the practice has evolved thanks to the internet, leveraging the vast digital space to create an impressive competitive playground.

2.1. Understanding the Basics

Affiliate marketing works on a simple principle. It involves promoting another company's products or services and earning a commission when purchases are made through your referral. As an affiliate marketer, your role involves selecting match-fit products, promoting them via your platform, and earning a fee for each sale that happens through your referral. What makes this model appealing is that you don't need to be involved in product creation or customer servicing.

2.2. Choosing the Ideal Product

Selecting the most suitable product to promote is pivotal to your success, and this requires adequate research. There are plenty of affiliate programs available, and the choices may overwhelm you. Narrowing down based on the industry, the product type, the reputation of the company, and the commission structure can guide your decision. Promoting the products that align with your platform and audience will lead to better conversions and, in turn, higher revenue.

2.3. Shaping Your Affiliate Marketing Strategy

A well-planned affiliate marketing strategy underscores the success of your endeavor. Your strategy outlines your goals, the products you'll be promoting, the channels you'll be using, and your targeted audience. It also dictates how you plan to drive traffic, generate clicks on your affiliate links, and convert visits into sales. A comprehensive understanding of digital marketing concepts such as Search Engine Optimization (SEO), Pay-Per-Click (PPC) advertising, content marketing, and social media marketing can significantly fuel your strategy.

2.4. Building Your Online Presence

In affiliate marketing, your online presence is your working desk. It could be a blog, a YouTube channel, a podcast, social media, or a combination of all of them. Your platform should provide valuable content that attracts and nurtures an audience interested in your niche. Building a strong online presence not only increases your chances of reaching your target audience but also gains trust, which is a significant factor in affiliate marketing.

2.5. Affiliate Marketing SEO

SEO is the lifeblood of affiliate marketing. Optimized content leads to better SERP rankings, attracting more traffic, and potentially more sales. A keyword-focused content strategy, combined with sound technical SEO practices like fast loading speeds, responsive design, and clean site architecture, can propel your site ranking.

2.6. The Art of Creating Persuasive Content

Content is king in the realm of affiliate marketing. Crafting content that answers your audience's needs and guides their decisions can be a game-changer. Your content should be persuasive enough to drive action but also realistic and relatable to build trust and credibility.

2.7. Conversions: The Ultimate Goal

Even with droves of traffic, success in affiliate marketing boils down to conversions. Tips like placing your affiliate links strategically, using compelling calls to action, and implementing website optimization techniques can improve your conversion rate. Tracking, testing, and tweaking are also integral parts of maximizing conversions.

2.8. Building Relationships

Affiliate marketing is not a one-time gig. It thrives on relationships. Building a relationship with your audience and maintaining healthy relationships with merchants is essential. Over time, these relationships translate into trust, which results in repeat sales and constant revenue.

2.9. Legal Considerations

While affiliate marketing presents a lucrative opportunity, it's crucial not to overlook the legal aspects. Having clarity on the terms and conditions of the affiliate program, understanding the regional advertising laws, and being transparent about your affiliate relationships are vital and non-negotiables.

Affiliate marketing isn't just about selling; it's a journey involving constant learning, strategic decision-making, and nurturing relationships. Met with the right approach and dedication, this potentially lucrative online marketing approach can lead to excellent wins.

Chapter 3. Blueprint for a Profitable Online Business

Welcome to the world of online entrepreneurship. This journey, while potentially lucrative, is one that requires a strategic approach, keen insight, as well as the flexibility to adapt and evolve. As we delve into creating a blueprint for a profitable online business, it's important to remember that success in this domain depends strongly on your ability to plan, act, and persevere.

3.1. Understanding Your Niche

Determining and understanding your niche is the first step to building a profitable online business. Your chosen niche should align with your passions and expertise, as this will help you connect with your target audience and deliver valuable content. An in-depth understanding of your target audience, their interests, needs, and pain points, is the key to crafting a compelling value proposition. This understanding will also help you identify the specific products or services within the affiliate programs that will address your target audience's needs and consequently result in sales conversions.

3.2. Selecting the Right Affiliate Program

The choice of an affiliate program can make or break your online business initiative. It's critical to pick affiliate programs that offer products or services that are relevant to your niche and audience. Consider factors such as commission structure, payout frequency, reputation of the brand, and the support provided by the program. Remember, the goal is to promote products that you believe in and that add value to your audience's lives.

3.3. Building a Robust Website

Your website will serve as the platform through which you interface with your audience. Therefore, investing in its design, user experience, and functionality is paramount. Start by choosing a domain name that reflects your brand and is easy for your intended audience to remember. Consider using an easy-to-navigate website layout that promotes discoveability of your content. Remember, the rule of thumb in successful affiliate marketing is to prioritize quality content over the sheer quantity of affiliate links.

3.4. Creating High-Quality Content

Content is the lifeblood of any affiliate marketing business. Your content should be original, engaging, and serve the purpose of helping your audience make informed buying decisions. This helps build trust and establishes you as an authority in your niche. Content can be presented in several formats - blog posts, tutorial videos, listicles, infographics, podcasts, among others. Remember to craft product reviews and informational guides that subtly weave in relevant affiliate products without coming across as salesy.

3.5. Mastering SEO

Search Engine Optimization (SEO) is an integral part of driving organic traffic to your website. By implementing SEO strategies such as keyword research and proper meta tags, you increase your site's visibility on search engine results pages (SERPs). SEO also involves optimizing your content layout, improving the site's loading speed, and ensuring your site is mobile-friendly - all these aimed to improve your audience's browsing experience.

3.6. Using Analytics to Your Advantage

Tracking and analyzing performance is crucial to the success of your online business. Tools like Google Analytics can provide valuable insights into your audience's behavior and preferences and reveal areas for improvement. You can identify which pieces of content perform well and which ones need tweaking. This feedback loop allows you to continuously adapt and grow your business.

3.7. Scaling Up

Once your online business is set up and generating a steady stream of income, it's time to consider scaling. This could involve diversifying your affiliate programs, replicating your successful strategies, outsourcing certain tasks, or even expanding into new niches. Remember, consistent growth requires continuous learning, testing, and iterating.

Building a profitable online business through affiliate marketing can be an exciting and rewarding venture. With the right mindset, dedication, and execution of the strategies outlined in this guide, you can turn your entrepreneurial dreams into reality. Remember to stay patient, however, as success may not come overnight. As the saying goes, 'Rome wasn't built in a day.' Enjoy the journey and all the learning that comes with it! Now go ahead and make your mark in the world of online entrepreneurship.

Chapter 4. Choosing the Right Niche for Success

To operate effectively in the vast, competitive landscape of affiliate marketing, identifying and choosing the proper niche is critical. It stands as the linchpin for your entire endeavor, potentially impacting the products you promote, the content you produce, and the audiences you target. In guidance, let's delve into the depths of what signifies a good niche and how to find one that resonates with your aspirations.

4.1. Understanding Niches

Fundamentally, a niche is a specialized market segment that targets a specific target audience with clear and unique needs. It is a small, defined, and meticulously tapped portion of a larger market. A niche market's primary definition is specificity—it's tailored to serve a distinct group or fill a distinct need. This can range from sellable items like gluten-free bread for health-conscious individuals or services targeted at dual-income parents with no time to clean their houses.

It's essential to understand how niches work because they can amplify your success in affiliate marketing. When you focus on a particular niche, you have fewer competitors to worry about. Moreover, you can better target your audience, making your marketing efforts more effective.

4.2. The Importance of the Right Niche

The niche you select will direct your entire affiliate marketing business, from the partnerships you form to the content you create and the audience you target. Consider these elements:

1. Product selection: Your chosen niche will significantly influence the products or services you can promote. A narrower focus can be better, allowing you to become an authority in that field, ultimately enhancing customer trust.

2. Audience targeting: Once you know your niche, it's easier to find and target your audience. You can understand their needs, preferences, and pain points, which is crucial in creating persuasive, compelling content.

3. Future growth: With the right niche, you can evolve and grow your business more effectively. It's quintessential to select a niche with promising growth potential and not just immediate profitability.

4.3. How to Identify a Profitable Niche

Now let's focus on the strategies for finding a profitable niche that aligns with your interests and skills, making your entrepreneurial journey a smooth sail.

First, list out your passions and interests. Starting with what you know or love can give you a head start, as your natural enthusiasm will reflect in your content, making it more engaging and authentic.

Secondly, you should identify the target market in those niches. Search for forums, blogs, and social media groups related to these interests to understand better the audience present and their needs.

Lastly, evaluate the profitability of your chosen niches. Do a competition analysis with tools like Google Keyword Planner or Semrush. You'll want to identify niches with high search volume but relatively low competition. Also, reckon the availability and diversity of affiliate products in your niche.

4.4. Understanding Your Audience

Understanding your target audience is crucial in choosing the right niche, as you'll be creating content and promoting products that cater to their needs and preferences.

Begin by building audience personas that reflect the demographic traits, interests, struggles, and desires of your potential consumers. Use tools like Google Analytics and social media analytics to gain insights.

Next, conduct surveys or host Q&A sessions in your niche communities. The feedback will enable you to evaluate if your products or services truly align with their needs and whether they're willing to pay for them.

Lastly, monitor your competitors. Assess their marketing tactics, engagement strategies, and customer feedback. This can provide pivotal insights into your audience's preferences and potential gaps in the market you could fill.

4.5. Final Thoughts on Selecting a Niche

If we were to encapsulate the essence of choosing a successful niche in affiliate marketing, it would be in understanding yourself, your audience, and the market. Your niche should ideally be at the intersection of your passion, market demand, and profitability.

Remember, no niche is perfect. There will be challenges and competition in any sector. But with thorough research, strategic planning, and genuine effort, you can transform any niche into a profitable endeavour. So, take your time in this crucial step. The result will be a strong foundation for your affiliate marketing business, ready to help you climb the ladder of online success.

Chapter 5. Mastering Affiliate Program Selection

Choosing the perfect affiliate program isn't just about signing up for the most popular one. It involves a careful analysis of several factors: the fit with your niche, payout terms, track record, and more. In this chapter, we'll deeply explore these aspects, ensuring that you're well-equipped to make the best choice.

5.1. Understanding Your Audience

The crux of affiliate marketing success begins with a comprehensive understanding of your audience. You need to have a clear picture of their interests, needs, and buying habits to effectively promote products that resonate with them. A good starting point is to conduct market research through surveys, social media interactions, and close monitoring of discussion forums and blog comments. Also take note of the kind of questions they're asking and problems they're looking to solve, as these can provide clues to the kinds of products and services they may be interested in.

5.2. Your Niche and Affiliate Program Compatibility

Once you understand your audience, examine your niche and the potential affiliate programs for compatibility. Look for programs that naturally align with your niche and will be an easy sell to your audience. This requires understanding the nature of the products or services being offered by the program. For example, if you run a fitness blog, an affiliate program selling gym equipment or nutritional supplements may be a perfect fit.

5.3. Examining the Affiliate Program's Reputation

Before committing to any affiliate program, make sure to evaluate its reputation. You can't afford to affiliate your website or business with a program that has a spotty track record. Do some research and look for reviews or feedback from other affiliates. Beware of programs with a history of late payments or poor customer service.

5.4. Payout Terms

Each affiliate program has different payout terms. Some programs offer a high percentage commission but with restrictive terms that could hurt your earning potential. Others might have lower commissions, but with favorable terms. Furthermore, consider the payment schedule. Some affiliate programs pay monthly, others quarterly, and others on a certain threshold. Make sure the payout terms align with your financial expectations and comfort levels.

5.5. Quality of Products or Services

Promoting high-quality products or services is crucial for the long-term viability of your online business. If the items you're endorsing are substandard, your audience will lose trust in your recommendations, reducing your chances of future sales. Always take time to personally vet the products or services you are promoting. Don't be afraid to ask for samples or demo access to understand what you will be selling.

5.6. Quality of Affiliate Support

A good affiliate program should also offer excellent affiliate support. This may include marketing tools such as banners and product images, training resources, and a dedicated team to handle any queries or issues that you may have. If the program doesn't support their marketers well, it's usually a red flag for other potential issues.

5.7. The Power of Diversification

Remember that putting all your eggs in one basket is not a great strategy in affiliate marketing. It's important to diversify your affiliate portfolio to increase your earnings and minimize risk. However, make sure you can effectively manage all of the programs you engage in and that each suits your niche.

5.8. Persist in Learning

The affiliate marketing landscape is very dynamic. New programs emerge and existing ones change their terms and conditions. Keep yourself in the loop about industry developments to ensure that you're always maximizing your potential earnings.

Selecting the right affiliate program is a journey of careful analysis, patience, and the constant pursuit of knowledge. Armed with these guidelines, you can make well-informed decisions that will significantly amplify your online business profitability. Remember, the key to mastery is through understanding and practice. As you take this knowledge and apply it to your affiliate marketing journey, you are taking powerful steps towards definite success.

Chapter 6. Creating an Affiliate Friendly Website

The backbone of your affiliate marketing strategy is a website that draws potential customers while ranking high in search engine results. In this section, we'll break down the essential elements for creating an affiliate friendly website.

=== The Importance of a Well-Designed Website

When customers visit your affiliate website, the design, layout, and functionality can significantly influence their shopping experience. The website should be easy to navigate, attractive, and mobile responsive. Good design prompts visitors to stay longer, explore more pages and has a higher chance of converting them into customers. Ideally, your website design should:

- Keep it simple: Avoid cluttering your website with unnecessary elements. Simplicity aids in clarity and usability.

- Consider mobile users: Always use a responsive design. This means your website adapts to the device it's being viewed on, which is vital as more than half of all web traffic now comes from mobile devices.

- Use attractive visuals: Visuals not only attract visitors but also make your website look professional. Ensure you use high-quality images related to your content.

- Use clear calls-to-action (CTAs): Make sure visitors know what action to take on your website. CTAs, such as "buy now," or "subscribe," should be in a prominent location on your page.

=== Keyword and SEO Optimisation

To attract organic traffic, your website needs to rank high in search engine results. This is where Search Engine Optimization (SEO) and keyword utilization come into play. SEO is a set of strategies that help websites reach higher positions in search engine results, making them more visible to potential customers.

You can practice good SEO by using the right keywords in your content. Your keyword selection should be based on what your target audience would likely use when searching for the products you promote. To find the best keywords for your affiliate marketing business, you can use keyword research tools like Google Keyword Planner, Moz Keyword Explorer, or SEMRush.

Remember to sprinkle these keywords throughout your content, but avoid overdoing it or "keyword stuffing." Keyword stuffing can lead to penalties from search engines, which can negatively impact your rankings.

=== Creating Quality Content

When it comes to affiliate marketing, content is king. High-quality content draws in visitors, keeps them on your site longer, and can even increase your website's ranking in search engine results.

The secret to creating good content lies in understanding your audience's needs and preferences. By understanding their problems and interests, you can create content that provides value, is engaging, and builds trust with your audience.

Suppose you are promoting kitchen appliances. In that case, you can create content like product reviews, how-to guides, recipes, or kitchen cleaning tips – anything that relates to your affiliate product and appeals to your audience.

Content can take many forms, not just written articles or blogs. You can experiment with videos, infographics, podcasts, or even webinars.

=== Affiliate Link Integration

Crucial to any affiliate website is the strategic placement of affiliate links. These links are what generate income as your site visitors click on them and hopefully make a purchase on the affiliated websites.

The golden rule for integrating affiliate links is transparency. Make sure your audience knows those are affiliate links, and outline it in a disclosure policy. Transparency helps in building trust among your audience.

When it comes to link placement, more is not always better. Overloading your website with affiliate links can make your site seem spammy, which can drive visitors away.

Optimal places for links include:

- Within your content: If relevant, embed a link in informational posts or review pieces.
- In the header or footer: Some brands may require that links stay visible and accessible from every page of your site. Headers and footers work excellently for this.

Remember to keep track of the clicks you get on your links to understand what works and what doesn't.

=== Website Tracking and Analytics

Setting up website tracking and analytics is crucial to understand your site's performance. Google Analytics, for instance, can provide in-depth information about your visitors, such as their location, the device they used, how much time they spent on your site, and which pages they visited.

With analytics, you can also measure the effectiveness of your SEO strategies, content, and affiliate links. If a particular type of content isn't attracting visitors, you can modify your strategy and focus on what works.

While these essential elements of an affiliate-friendly website can help lay the foundation for your online venture, the most critical aspect will always be consistent experimentation, learning, and evolution. Keep improving and tweaking, and surely, success will come in due course.

Next, we'll delve into some advanced strategies on how to find the best affiliate networks and succeed. Stay tuned!

Chapter 7. Driving High Quality Traffic

Fundamental to making your mark in the affiliate marketing domain is the ability to drive high-quality traffic to your affiliate links. Only when there's substantial traffic, will there be chances of conversions leading to your commission earnings. Let's discuss some effective strategies to boost your affiliate marketing game through effective traffic generation.

7.1. Understand Your Target Audience

Understanding your audience is at the apex of priorities when it comes to driving quality traffic. Be aware of their interests, needs, and online behavior to align your marketing strategies accordingly. Ascertain what content resonates most with them, the solutions they're seeking, and how they prefer interacting with online content.

Audience interaction can be tracked with tools like Google Analytics that offer valuable insights into the demographics, interests, behavior, and other crucial data about your audience. By analyzing this information, you can tailor your content to be more attractive and engaging for your target segment.

7.2. Content Marketing for Affiliate Campaigns

Your content is the primary bridge between your audience and the affiliate products you're promoting. It's imperative to ensure that it's engaging, informational, and compelling. Guide your audience through your content, subtly blending in your affiliate links where they fit naturally.

Write blogs or articles related to your affiliate products and optimize them for search engines (Search Engine Optimization). This not only brings organic traffic to your website but also establishes your authority in the specific niche. The more value you're providing through your content, the higher the chances that the audience will trust your product recommendations.

7.3. SEO: A Cornerstone Strategy

SEO is a must-implement tactic for driving high-quality traffic. Implementing SEO strategies will make your content discoverable through search engines and help carve your web presence. The use of the right keywords, link-building, on-page SEO (using meta tags, proper URL structure) and off-page SEO (social media marketing, influencer marketing) can significantly increase your SERPs, leading to more organic traffic.

Use tools like Google Keyword Planner or Semrush to identify the keywords your potential customers might be using. Ensure that your content is structured around these keywords without stuffing them forcibly.

7.4. Email Marketing

Email marketing remains one of the most effective methods for driving quality traffic. Building an email list allows you to maintain direct contact with your potential customers. You can periodically send them information about new affiliate products, offers, and other helpful content.

Using an engaging Call-To-Action (CTA), you can encourage your site visitors to subscribe to your email list. Once they're in, provide them consistent value, maintain communication, and avoid overt sales pitches.

7.5. Utilizing Social Media Platforms

Present on virtually every social media platform, your potential customers offer a rich source of traffic. Use these platforms to share affiliate links directly or drive traffic to your content containing the affiliate links. Whether it's Instagram, Facebook, Twitter or Pinterest, knowing where your audience hangs out the most is crucial.

Create engaging posts, interact with your followers regularly, and provide useful content. Adopt the strategy of influencer marketing by collaborating with popular figures in your niche could generate more traffic and sales.

7.6. Running Paid Ad Campaigns

If budget permits, leveraging paid advertising platforms like Google AdWords, Bing Ads, or social media ads can significantly speed up your traffic generation process. Before diving in, take time to understand each platform's various ad formats and targeting capabilities.

Paid advertising can direct highly specific traffic to your websites. Use the tracking data provided by these platforms to optimize your campaigns and get improved results over time.

7.7. Affiliate Marketing Forums and Communities

Utilize affiliate marketing specific forums and communities like Affilorama, Warrior Forum, or Reddit's affiliate marketing thread. They can offer tremendous opportunities for collaboration, learning, and traffic generation.

Remember, in these forums, it's not about bombarding everyone with your affiliate links. Instead, provide value first, establish your expertise, and naturally weave in your links when they fit the context.

Driving high-quality traffic is the lifeblood of your affiliate marketing business. Each strategy discussed is a strong traffic driver when used correctly. However, adapting them to suit your specific business needs and consistent fine-tuning for optimal results remains an integral part of the process. Stay committed to providing superior content and value to your audience, and see your affiliate marketing venture thrive.

Chapter 8. Converting Traffic into Sales

In the realm of affiliate marketing, the copious inflow of visitors to your website symbolizes potential prosperity, granted that their curiosity transforms into purchases. Your website, akin to a storefront, demands strategic display of goods, persuasive interaction and utmost credibility to successfully convince your website traffic to evolve from visitors to customers.

8.1. The Power of Credibility

For any affiliate marketing enterprise, trust forms the bedrock of conversion. Potential buyers are likely to make a purchase if your product reviews or recommendations are honest, detailed and come from a point of experience or deep understanding. Rather than flaunting every single product available under your affiliate network, focus on promoting the ones you've tested, used or have verifiable understanding of. To achieve credibility:

- Provide in-depth product reviews detailing the benefits and drawbacks to allow potential buyers to make informed decisions.

- Include personal testimonials and case studies where possible to demonstrate the usefulness of the product.

- Consistently update content to keep parity with the ever-evolving market trends, ensuring your content remains relevant and thereby credible.

8.2. Crafting a Persuasive Call to Action (CTA)

A strategically crafted call-to-action persuades your audience to take the desired action and finalize the purchase. A good CTA:

- Is clear, specific, and emits a sense of urgency.
- Is well positioned on your website, ideally both at the top and bottom of product reviews or comparisons.
- Uses attractive colors that stand out from the rest of the webpage.

8.3. Conversion Tracking

Follow the trends. Monitor which links attract more clicks and lead to a higher number of sales. Implement conversion tracking tools, such as Google Analytics. This can provide rich insights into your user behavior, inform future strategies and possibly detect loopholes in your current ones.

8.4. The Enchantment of Content

Valuable and engaging content can convert the most indecisive of your visitors. Make sure your content:

- Adds value by being full of useful product-related information that solves a problem or fulfills a need.
- Is interesting enough to make your visitors want to read more, returning for more such content.
- Is shared across all your marketing channels – blogs, newsletters, social media – to create awareness and attract more potential buyers.

8.5. Email Marketing

Another excellent method to convert your traffic into sales is through email marketing. By encouraging your visitors to subscribe to your email list, you can create a treasure trove of potential customers. Personalized and valuable emails can lead to better relationships with customers, which in turn boost your conversion rates.

To swiftly make the most out of your email marketing, ensure to:

- Provide compelling incentives for users to subscribe to your list.
- Send regular, relevant and engaging emails to spark interest among your subscribers.
- Promote special offers exclusively to your email subscribers before launching on other channels.

8.6. Landing Page Optimization

Crafting a smooth, enjoyable and easy-to-navigate user experience on your landing page can greatly increase your conversion rates. This includes obvious but crucial factors such as page loading speed, stunning visuals, and intuitive navigation.

Moreover, landing page personalization – which involves creating tailored experiences for different segments of your audience – can significantly help in converting the traffic into sales. A/B testing your landing pages can be invaluable here, as it can help you understand what works and what doesn't for your specific audience.

8.7. Customer Retention

While attracting and converting new customers is vital, retaining existing customers should not be overlooked. Happy and loyal customers can contribute heavily to consistent revenue and may aid in attracting new customers via word of mouth.

Ensure to keep your customers satisfied by:

- Providing top-notch customer service.
- Sending personalized offers that make them feel valued.
- Engaging them through relatable and interactive content.

In conclusion, converting traffic into sales is not mathematically calculated but it is thoughtfully cultivated. Employing effective strategies like enhancing credibility, crafting persuasive CTAs, providing exceptional content, leveraging email marketing, optimizing landing pages, and strongly focusing on customer retention can significantly escalate your sales and cement your success in the arena of online entrepreneurship. The incredible financial independence that comes with mastering these techniques is no longer far-fetched. As you mold these strategies to suit your unique business requirements, remember that an affiliate marketer's true success lies in persistent efforts, continuous learning, and tireless ingenuity.

Chapter 9. Search Engine Optimization Tactics for Affiliates

SEO, or Search Engine Optimization, is a crucial aspect of any online marketing, and it's no different for affiliates. This practice revolves around enhancing a website's visibility in search engine results pages (SERPS), thereby driving organic (free) traffic to your site. The high quality traffic you can pull in, the higher your chances of converting these individuals into customers or, in the context of affiliate marketing, referral clients.

9.1. Understanding SEO and Its Importance

SEO can look intimidating initially, particularly to individuals who have never encountered the term. However, upon accurate recognition, you'll see that it's an all-encompassing term for various strategies used to boost a site's visibility on search engines like Google and Bing. The primary goal here is to heighten the quantity and quality of internet traffic your website receives.

For affiliate marketers, boosting website visibility is essential to facilitate more people to see your affiliate offers. Remember that no matter how terrific your offers might be, they're ineffective if they don't reach your desired audience. Good SEO practices can aid you in targeting the correct demographic, leading to increased conversions and, in due course, better profits.

9.2. Keywords: The Cornerstone of SEO

Keywords are the bedrock upon which successful SEO strategies are built. These are phrases or words that your target audience utilizes when searching online for products, services, or information. In affiliate marketing, effective keyword research can help you determine what products or niches are in high demand and how to best position your site and offers to meet that demand.

There are numerous tools (free and paid) available online for keyword research, such as Google Keyword Planner, Ubersuggest, and SEMrush. SEO emphasizes on highlighting the right keywords, the ones that your potential audience uses to find the products or services that you promote.

9.3. On-Page SEO Tactics for Affiliates

On-page SEO steers on the optimization of on-site elements. This optimization can range from the incorporation of your chosen keywords into strategic areas to the structure of your site's content.

- Keyword Placement: Make sure your chosen keywords seamlessly blend into your titles, headings, meta descriptions, URLs, and content. However, avoid falling into the 'keyword stuffing' trap, which can lead to penalties from search engines.

- Content Quality: Ensure that your site provides high-quality content that is relevant and engaging. Your content should offer value to the user, answering their queries and providing beneficial information.

- Site Structure: Keep your website structured in a manner that's easy to navigate, with each page accessible in a few clicks from the homepage. This usability factor impacts SEO positively.

9.4. Off-Page SEO Tactics for Affiliates

Off-page SEO focuses on actions taken outside of your own website, impacting your site's trustworthiness, relevance, and authority. These tactics primarily involve link-building strategies, as search engines utilize backlinks (hyperlinks on other websites that point to your site) as indicators of your site's credibility.

- Backlink Building: There are varied approaches to this, such as guest posting, article marketing, and so on. The key here is to secure backlinks from sites relevant to your niche and having high domain authority.

- Social Signals: Although not a direct ranking factor, social signals (likes, shares, tweets, pins, etc.) can assist in boosting your site's organic traffic. Sharing buttons for social media on your site can facilitate the process.

9.5. Local SEO for Affiliates

Local SEO involves the optimization of your online presence to attract more customers from relevant local searches. As an affiliate marketer, even if your offerings are not location-specific, it might still be beneficial to target certain geographical locations depending on the nature of your affiliate products.

- Google My Business: Start by listing your business on 'Google My Business' and optimizing the listing with relevant information, photos, reviews, etc.

- Reviews: Encourage reviews from users who have benefited from your recommendations. This will build your credibility and transparency in the eyes of the visitors.

9.6. Tracking the Right SEO Metrics

To gauge the effectiveness of your SEO strategies, you need to track the right metrics. Some essential ones include:

- Organic Traffic: This is the primary gauge of whether your SEO tactics are working. Use analytics tools to examine this metric.

- Bounce Rate: If this rate is too high, it indicates that users are not finding what they are looking for on your site, and you may need to audit your content or site design.

- Conversion Rate: As an affiliate marketer, conversions can translate into successful affiliate sales. Keeping an eye on this metric can provide insight into how effectively your site compels visitors to take the desired action.

While SEO may seem overwhelming initially, understanding its various elements can provide a solid foundation for your affiliate marketing efforts. Applying conscientious SEO tactics can substantially increase your site's visibility, drawing more qualified traffic, and in turn, escalating conversions. As an affiliate marketer, your success depends on these conversions. Thus, mastering SEO should be a priority in your affiliate marketing journey.

Chapter 10. Harnessing the Power of Social Media

Understanding the dynamics of social media is pivotal in developing successful affiliate marketing campaigns. Different social platforms harbor various demographic groups, each with their distinctive tastes and interests. Knowing where your target audience congregates, their behaviors, and preferences can provide crucial insights that will guide your social media strategy.

10.1. Identifying Your Target Audience

Begin by defining who your ideal client is. Demographic factors like age, gender, location, interests, and occupations are key points to understand. For instance, if you're promoting a gaming product, your primary audience might be younger individuals who show interest in gaming.

Various social media platforms offer insights about their users. Facebook's Audience Insights Tool, for instance, provides a wealth of information about your audience's interests, behaviors, and more. Twitter Analytics offers similar features. Use these tools to your benefit to refine your target audience.

10.2. Picking the Right Platform

While Facebook and Instagram cater more to visual content and serve a wide range of audiences, Twitter's fast-paced environment is better suited for instant updates and LinkedIn appeals to the professional market.

For your affiliate marketing efforts, you need to choose a platform where your target audience is most likely to be active. If your product is visually appealing and best demonstrated through images or videos, Instagram might be your best choice. If it appeals to professionals, then LinkedIn is where you want to be.

10.3. Crafting Compelling Social Media Content

Content is the backbone of any social media marketing venture. For your posts to convert, they need to be valuable, relevant, and engaging. Compelling content will encourage your followers to click on your affiliate links.

Informational posts, infographics, tutorials, webinars, live Q&As, case studies, and stories of personal experiences are excellent content forms that can both inform and engage your followers. They need to see that your content is more than affiliate links–it's beneficial and valuable to them.

10.4. Utilizing Social Media Tools

Harnessing the power of social media tools can aid in streamlining your affiliate marketing efforts. For instance, scheduling tools like Buffer and Hootsuite allow you to plan and schedule your posts for peak engagement times. Tools like Followerwonk can help you understand your followers' behaviors further.

Using link shortening services like Bitly not only makes your posts look cleaner but also provides you with analytics to understand which posts get the most engagement and conversions.

10.5. Social Media Advertising

While organic efforts are essential in building trust and

relationships, social media advertising allows you to widen your reach and target individuals outside your followers.

Facebook Ads Manager and Instagram Advertising allow you to create custom audiences based on demographics, interests, and behaviors. This ensures your content reaches the right people, increasing the likelihood of conversions.

10.6. Leveraging User-Generated Content

User-generated content (UGC) can be a powerful way to engage your audience and build social proof. Encourage your audience to share posts about your product or service, tagging your account, or using a unique hashtag. By sharing these posts on your account, you can create a sense of community and authenticity.

10.7. Engaging With Your Audience

Interacting with your followers makes them feel valuable and heard. Respond to comments, direct messages, and posts about your product or service. Simple gestures like thanking a customer for their feedback or solving a minor issue can go a long way in cultivating loyal followers.

10.8. Staying Updated

Social media platforms are evolving fast, and keeping up with these changes is integral for your affiliate marketing success. Regularly educate yourself about new features, tools, platforms, and trends in your industry to stay one step ahead.

Remember, social media is a powerful tool in the affiliate marketer's toolkit. Properly harnessed, it can drive significant traffic to your affiliate links, resulting in robust conversions and revenue streams. Thus, leverage it wisely and watch your online venture flourish.

Chapter 11. Navigating the Pitfalls and Maximizing Profits

No journey to success is without its trials and tribulations; the path to affiliate marketing mastery is no different. This journey, although laden with golden opportunities for high profits, is also beset with myriad pitfalls that are capable of derailing your aspirations for financial prosperity. This chapter heeds your concerns and walks you through effective strategies to navigate the pitfalls and to furbish your profit-maximizing prowess.

11.1. Understanding the Potential Pitfalls

To navigate the pitfalls skillfully, we must first identify and understand them. Affiliate marketing, like any other business, presents a number of challenges and risks.

11.1.1. Over-reliance on One Marketing Channel

A common mistake is to put all your marketing eggs in one basket. A sudden change in the algorithm of a traffic source or loss of rank on a single platform could see a dramatic drop in your income. It's wise to diversify your traffic sources for sustainability.

11.1.2. Promoting Poor Quality Products

Choosing to promote low-quality products can put you in a precarious position. Your reputation is at stake every time you recommend a product. If it's subpar, your credibility takes a hit, and you'll lose your audience's trust. Therefore, it's always better to vet the products you promote.

11.1.3. Non-compliance to Rules and Regulations

Every affiliate program comes with specific rules and regulations. Failure to adhere to them can lead to account suspensions or even a complete ban from the program. Always read and respect the guidelines of your chosen affiliate program.

11.1.4. Lack of Patience and Consistency

Affiliate marketing is not a get-rich-quick scheme. To yield a substantial and sustainable income, it demands patience, consistency, and dedication.

11.2. Strategies to Maximize Profits

Having a clear understanding of the potential pitfalls, let's now focus on the strategies you can implement to maximize your earnings in affiliate marketing.

11.2.1. Choose the Right Affiliate Products

The first key to maximizing profits lies in selecting the right products. You'll want to choose products that are relevant to your audience, have a decent commission rate, and have a good reputation in the marketplace. Always know what you're promoting and be confident in the product's value.

11.2.2. Leverage SEO

While paid advertisements can bring immediate traffic, search engine optimization (SEO) can bring in organic, and potentially more sustainable, traffic over time. Implementing effective SEO strategies such as keyword optimization, quality linkage, and unique content creation can significantly augment your visibility in search engine results, thereby driving more traffic to your site.

11.2.3. Grow and Nurture your Email List

Building and nurturing your email list can be hugely beneficial for your affiliate marketing business. It allows you to establish a direct line of communication with your audience. Regularly send them valuable content to strengthen your relationship and build their trust. When trust is in place, you have a better chance of converting these contacts into customers.

11.2.4. Implement Tracking and Analytics Tools

Make use of tracking and analytics tools to understand what works and what doesn't. These tools can provide valuable insights into your audience's behavior, letting you optimize your content and approach to better resonate with them.

Continuous learning is integral to your success. As algorithms change and trends shift, make sure you adapt and evolve to keep pace with the changing landscapes of the online business world. Your ability to weather the challenges and maximize profits will determine your affiliate marketing mastery.

So, let the odyssey of online entrepreneurship be a brave journey of learning, exploration, and advancement. It might be fraught with obstacles, but remember that within each challenge lies a greater opportunity for growth and prosperity.

www.ingramcontent.com/pod-product-compliance
Lightning Source LLC
Chambersburg PA
CBHW062311290526
45794CB00006B/2760